And The
CHILD
GREW

A contemporary follow-up
manual for new believers

Ernest C. Uzoho

And the Child Grew

English
Copyright @2010
Revised Edition, 5th Printing, 2017
ISBN 978-978-49970-4-1

Unless otherwise stated, all scripture quotations are from New King James Version of the Bible.

A MIREN Publication.
Ten Thousand copies in circulation

Property of
Mission Rescue Evangelistic Network
(MIREN)
World Mission Centre, New Road Location
Off Ada George Road, Port Harcourt, Nigeria. +234-803 351 0455, +234-803 715 7294

Email: mirenhq@gmail.com

Dedication

I watch him grow, Ihendu my son. I desired that in him, the gospel of Jesus Christ will have a mightier expression, sustaining the light of life as his name is. As I watch him grow in body and in wisdom, I desire that he may also grow in spirit, and in the love of God, unto manhood, in the Kingdom of our Lord Jesus Christ, the Son of God. I will see him become useable and useful in the hands of the Lord by virtue of his graceful growth in Christ.

To Graham Ihendu my son, I dedicate this little book, and to all who gave their lives to Christ in our Freedom and Healing Crusades around Africa.

Introduction

I have been in the fore- front of soul winning and evangelism for more than two decades. I was introduced to this crucial ministry immediately after my conversion at age thirteen.

All these years, I can never forget the glorious and eternal impact the believers class made in my spiritual walk with God at that new beginning. I owe everything of my ministry today to those foundational classes, and to those men, my tutors, who knew much of God in their hearts than our modern scholars know in their heads.

The values a man will hold most sacred after his conversion are the values he is introduced to within two months of his or her conversion, beginning from not later than 46 hours after his conversion.

Today, the missing link between half-baked, busy-life, city Christianity and primitive spirit-filled Christianity is this bed rock-New Believers Class.

It is an irony that people are converted into the great faith, and the first doctrines they hear is power, anointing and prosperity. This is jump starting. Everything that jump starts has the tendency of knocking.

By my direct contact with hundreds of thousands of new believers in our mission fields and crusades around the world ,I feel the necessity laid on me to produce a handy work that will serve as a personal guide to the new convert. This necessary burden was doubled when once my wife Chidinma, in one of our executive meetings asked us a worrisome question. She asked and said, what happens to our new converts when we leave the mission field or crusade? Can we trust their sustain ability to those indigenous pastors? Moreso she introduced a new lexicon to our evangelical vocabulary when she further said - we need to develop a retainship spirit for this new converts. We in the Network understood every meaning of that word retainship to us it means ABILITY TO KEEP. That retainer ship spirit is what has produced this work.

That retainship spirit is what has produced this work.

This booklet is designed to be interactive, simple and friendly. By this, it will eliminate boredom from the reader and communicate values in a very simple but penetrating manner.

I believe that this work will please the Lord, and decrease the number of "falling aways" while increasing the retainship spirit of the new believers.

1 THE NEW BIRTH

What is the new birth? The new birth is a tangible spiritual transformative experience that a person experiences at the moment he or she wholly surrenders his/her life to Jesus Christ. At that time we say he or she is born again. The Spirit of God is responsible for this new birth in man. The new birth is the incoming of eternal life unto a man. When we get the new birth, we get eternal life. Man is totally lost in sin, doomed unto eternal damnation. Even a baby that is born today has sin in his streams by nature. The sin of Adam is a sin of all mankind. It is the original sin. It goes through the blood of all people. We are condemned just by being human beings. Death flows through our lives by that.

> "Therefore, just as through one man sin entered the world, and death through sin, and thus

death spread to all men, because all sinned." Romans 5:12

However, Jesus Christ brought eternal life to stop this long Adamic sin trend. That eternal life is what we receive through the new birth. "For as in Adam all die, even so in Christ all shall be made alive." 1Corinthians 15:22

We received this eternal life immediately we surrender to Jesus. The Bible puts it this way;

> "For God so loved the world that He gave His only begotten Son, that whoever believes in Him should not perish but have everlasting life." John 3:16

This eternal life we receive at new birth is the life of God that will everlastingly stop the flow of eternal death brought upon us by Adam's sin.

How Does One Receive The New Birth?
There was this man, so learned; he could even be called a professor. He was also an experienced man, a ruler. He knew a lot of things, but he did not know how to receive the new birth. His name is Nicodemus. He asked Jesus a question saying "How can a man be

born again?" That is to say "how can a man have the new birth?" Jesus answered him saying, "Except a man be born of water and of the Spirit, he cannot enter the kingdom of God".

What does it mean to be born of water and to be born of the Spirit?
Apostle Paul later made us understand what the water herein means. Water is used for cleansing. Jesus symbolically used water to demonstrate how the word of God can cleanse us from that adamic stain. The water is the word of God you heard which is able to cleanse you.

> "That He might sanctify and cleanse her with the washing of water by the word." Ephesians 5:26

To be born of water is to receive the word of God which has the power to cleanse us from all unrighteousness. The Spirit herein means the convicting Spirit of God. Except a man has heard the Word of God and he is convicted by the convicting Spirit of God he cannot see the Kingdom of God. Except that same Spirit dwells in the man, he cannot see the Kingdom of God.

Assurance of Salvation

If you are on transit with a computer set, or a television set, and you are confronted by a police officer on check point. If the police officer requires who owns what you are carrying, you will of course reply that it is yours. Then, he asks the second question "where is the proof that this computer or television set belongs to you?" At that time, you have one authentic proof to show you own it. You put your hand in your pocket, bring out a little paper, and hand it over to the police saying "this is the receipt" at that time, all arguments ends.
question "where is the proof that this computer or television set belongs to you?" At this point, you have one authentic proof to show you own it. You put your hand in your pocket, bring out a little paper, and hand it over to the police man saying "this is the receipt" with this, all arguments ends.

In that same manner, if Satan confronts you on your way and say "who are you?" and you reply "I am a new birth, a born again Christian, a new creature."

Then he will ask, "How are you sure?" "How can you proof it?" At that time, what will you do?

Herein, I am handling over six authentic proofs to you that you are now a Christian, that you are saved, that your sins are forgiven, that you are a child of God.

NUMBER 1 ASSURANCE: The Bible says so! In 2 Corinthians 5:17, it says:

> "Therefore, if anyone is in Christ, he is a new creation; old things have passed away; behold, all things have become new."

This is what the word of God says. This is an all powerful assurance, that you are now a new person, a new soul; every other old conduct and judgment are passed away. You are now a new creature.

> "Most assuredly, I say to you, he who hears My word, and believes in Him who sent Me has everlasting life, and shall not come into judgment, but has passed from death into life."
> John 5:24

NUMBER 2 ASSURANCE: Witness of the Spirit

With every new creature, (every person that just surrenders his life to Jesus Christ is a new creature), such a person has the Spirit of God in him. The spirit in the inside of him speaks gently to him inwardly saying- "you are now changed", "you are a new person", "you are now a Christian", "you are born again". He says this softly and internally. This is what we call the witness of the spirit. He bears witness to you the same way he convicts you when you sin that what you are doing is wrong; but now he tells you, "You are on the right track." The word of God puts it this way: a new person", "you are now a Christian", "you are born again". He says this softly and internally. This is what we call the witness of the spirit. He bears witness to you the same way he convicts you when you sin that what you are doing is wrong; but now he tells you, "You are on the right track." The word of God puts it this way:

> "For you did not receive the spirit of bondage again to fear, but you received the Spirit of adoption by whom we cry out, "Abba, Father." The Spirit Himself bears witness with our spirit that we are children of God." Romans 8:15-16

Is your spirit testifying to you that you are now born again? If yes, bless God!

NUMBER 3 ASSURANCE: Joy of Salvation
There is this experience every truly born again believer experiences. It is an internal bubbling of Joy. It is a joy that is not attached to material things, but you will soon discover that you are joyous in your inside. Sometimes

you see yourself singing in your heart and feeling very happy as though some body gave you something. That is what is called the joy of salvation.

When David (the beloved of the Lord) sinned against God, the Lord took this joy of salvation away from him and he cried saying:
> "Restore to me the joy of Your salvation, and uphold me by Your generous Spirit." Psalms 51:12

This joy of salvation is so important that David could not wait a minute when it departed to ask God to restore it. If you don't have it, ask God to give it to you now. It is your right. It is your assurance number 2 that you are bon again. The Bible puts it this:
It this way;
> "Therefore with joy you will draw water from the wells of salvation." Isaiah 12:3

Declaration: Lay your right hand on your chest and say:
> "With Joy I shall draw water out of the wells of salvation, and this my joy in the Holy Spirit shall not run dry, in Jesus name."

What does it mean to draw water from the wells of salvation? You remembered what I told you before that water is the word of God.

It means then that as you encounter the saving word of God, you will find new things about God and joy shall so much fill your heart, that it will be like a river flowing in your heart!

NUMBER 4 ASSURANCE: Peace with God

Do you remember that song that says; "It is well, it is well with my soul"
This song was sung by a man who had peace with God. He was a born again Christian on transit, on the high sea. He got a telegram that his children got drawn in the pool as they went to swim. All his children died! Instead of him to begin to blame God, he erupted in glorious songs to exalt God. That is another kind of internal peace. One strong witness that you are now saved is that you have peace towards God. Before, you may not feel free to go to such places like prayer meetings, fasting programmes, night vigils and so on. Before you don't like to know pastors, because you feel they will tell you something about your bad life. Suddenly, in this your new experience you now have peace in yourself with God and all these divine things you formally abhorred, you now begin to adore and enjoy them.
 That is what it means to have peace with God.
The Bible talks about it this way saying:

> "Therefore, having been justified by faith, we have peace with God through our Lord Jesus Christ" Romans 5:1

Some people, before they became saved, they cannot sleep in the night. They are always afraid, always afraid of one thing or the other. Some feel so frightened by what they have done against men and God that they can't just sleep at night. But immediately you get Christ inside of you, He gives you peace. Whenever you begin to feel that peace, it is an assurance that truly, you are saved. Jesus is the One and only One that gives us that peace, that inner tranquility. See how he puts it:

> "Peace I leave with you, My peace I give to you; not as the world gives do I give to you. Let not your heart be troubled, neither let it be afraid." John 14:27

I have a question for you, since you got born again have you experienced peace within you? If your answer is yes, then that peace means your soul has finally come to satisfaction, that you are now saved. Hallelujah!

NUMBER 5 ASSURANCE: Witness of Men

When you get the new birth, it is so obvious that people around you will begin to see a different thing in you. They will begin to observe your change in attitude. Suddenly the people close to you will begin to observe you closely, saying things like "you have changed." Some will say, "There is something new about you." While others will boldly ask you, "are you now born again?" These are all good witnesses of men. When men begin to witness that you have changed, that is a real assurance that you have changed indeed. People will observe that you have Christ in you. They will know that you now have fellowship with the Son of God. Do you know that when the Disciples of Christ got saved, people noticed it? When they preached to the people; the priests, the captain of the temple and the Sadducees arrested them, and brought them to judgment. But as the disciples spoke in the council, the people were shocked by their sudden boldness to speak and their new behavior. Previously, the disciples used to be timid and will never openly accept that they were Christians, but immediately they became bold and spoke God's word with boldness. The Bible says concerning that:

Disciples of Christ got saved, people noticed it? When they preached to the people; the priests, the captain of the temple and the

Sadducees arrested them, and brought them to judgment. But as the disciples spoke in the council, the people were shocked by their sudden boldness to speak and their new behaviour. Previously, the disciples used to be timid and will never openly accept that they were Christians, but immediately they became bold and spoke God's word with boldness. The Bible says concerning that:

> "Now when they saw the boldness of Peter and John, and perceived that they were uneducated and untrained men, they marveled. And they realized that they had been with Jesus."
> Acts 4:13

So when people begin to talk about you that you are now behaving "church, church" - Be happy, it is the witness of men that you have the new birth.

NUMBER 6   ASSURANCE :Change of Desire

Sin is an appetite. When it comes upon a man, he will want to get satisfied by indulging in it. The appetite of lust leads to sexual immorality. Some have the appetite to quarrel, to fight, to abuse, to steal, to cheat, to lie, and commit all other vices. Some are hot tempered. However, when you get saved, you will discover that suddenly, the wanton

Exercise

1 What is the new birth?

....

....

....

....

....

2. Who is responsible for this new birth?

....

....

3. Complete this sentence: "the ....….. of
Adam is the ....….................. of all mankind.
4. What does it mean to be born of the Water?

....

....

....

....

....

5. List five authentic assurances of your salvation.
(i) ....…...................….................
(ii) ....
(iii)...…...............
(iv) ....…......................
(v)..…......................

2 | OVERCOMING TEMPTATION

Do you know that temptation is not sin? It is yielding to temptation that is sin! The Bible says that Satan tempted Jesus Christ with three major things; The lust of the eye, the pride of life, and the desire of the flesh. You will meet Jesus temptations in Matthew chapter 4 from verse 1 to verse11.

Often, I hear new converts cry and say- "the devil is always tempting me!" they forget that the same devil tempted Jesus, and will tempt every believer to test and see if they are genuinely saved. According to Matthew's account, the first temptation Satan tempted Jesus was to find out if He had mastered and conquered His lust of the flesh. Satan said to Him: "If you are the Son of God, command that these stones become bread." Matthew 4:3

Satan knew Jesus was hungry at that time, so he brought the lust of the flesh to tempt Him. Some people's lust of the flesh temptation may be when they are in need of their husband or wife, and maybe the spouse is away on a course. Satan brings another option "You need warmth and love, don't you? Why not sleep with this ready man available since you can't reach your spouse?" This kind of temptation is lust of the flesh. Another example of lust of the flesh is having sin partners in the name of boyfriend or girlfriend.

You may be so much in need of money, very critical need of money, and an opportunity to make handsome money through fraud shows up. The devil catches in on your need of money at that time and says to you, "You know you need money, if you don't get this money now, things will spoil, why not get this money through this trick, and nobody will know, nobody, not even a soul!" This is temptation, and God watches how you will wangle out of it.

Some people may be in an exam hall, suddenly the invigilator brings to you the answers and says "take this expo, and write quickly and pass, you know this is your last chance". That is temptation, we all passed through it and survived, and you too will pass through it and survive. One funny thing with temptation is that when it comes, it seems it is the only chance you have to survive. That is a lie of the devil. What did Jesus do to His own temptation? He remembered what the word of God says about it, and having armed Himself with that powerful Word of God, He quoted it out to the devil saying:

"It is written, Man shall not live by bread alone, but by every Word that proceeds from the mouth of God." Matthew 4: 4

You see, it is very important for you to know what the Word of God says. That is why you should be in the habit of reading the Bible. If Jesus did not know what the Word of God says, He would have fallen to the devil. Remember what the Word of God says and use it against the devil.

Why Am I tempted?

Temptation is a test of faith every child of God must pass through. You are tempted because Satan wants to discourage your faith. He wants to know if you truly mean business with God by leaving his (Satan's) fold. Temptations look outwardly nice to fall into, but are deadly when a child of God falls into it. Satan is the chief tempter, he does that through his demons and men that are not spiritually conscious.

Does God tempt?

Many times, you hear new converts say "God is tempting me, He wants me to fall". But does God really tempt any one? God does not tempt, because God cannot bring sin to you and desire you fall into it. Satan is the one that brings sin to you, and desires you fall into it. But God can TRY you by demanding of you to take an action of faith or endure hard times. The difference between trials and temptations are:

You to take an action of faith or endure hard times. The difference between trials and temptations are:

Trials	Temptations
Trials are designed to increase your faith	Temptations are designed to extinguish your faith
Trials come from God or allowed by God	Temptations come from the devil, and never from God
We are tried with circumstances of life	We are tempted with sin
Trials come to proof our assignment	Temptations come to proof our lust.

Do you know that it is our lust that brings temptation to us? God does not tempt, but our lust brings temptation to us. Look at how the Bible says it:

"Let no one say when he is tempted, 'I am tempted by God',' for God cannot be tempted by evil, nor does He Himself tempt anyone. But each one is tempted when he is drawn away by his own desires and enticed." James 1:13-14

You see it here; it is our lust that brings us into temptation. If you are someone that has lust for sex for instance, Satan will then tempt you with that. If you are so desirous of money, Satan will then tempt you with that. Satan cannot tempt you with what you do not have desire for. So, for us to avoid and overcome temptation, we must kill our lust and wanton desires. If you are quick tempered, Satan will tempt you with anger. So when you become born again, the first thing you do is to begin to renew your mind, because it is in your mind that all the adamic lust resides. That is why the Bible says:

> *"Do not love or cherish the world or the things that are in the world. If anyone loves the world, love for the Father is not in him. For all that is in the world the lust of the flesh [craving for sensual gratification] and the lust of the eyes [greedy longings of the mind] and the pride of life [assurance in one's own resources or in the stability of earthly things]- these do not come from the Father but are from the world* [itself]." 1ˢᵗ John 2:15-16 (Amplified version)

To avoid temptation, the Bible tells us not to love the world, isn't it? Then if that is what it says, what does it mean by the world?

There was a time some Christians use to call television, "devil's box".Some Christians call fine cars "carnality". Some call chain watches "worldliness". Are these things what the Bible means by the world? If that is what the Bible means by the world, then we will practically condemn everything that is in the world including our Bibles, because the Word of God is printed on earthly papers. The papers used in printing the Bible are from the world!

The Lord knew this kind of misconceptions about what the world is will arise, so the meaning was explicitly explained. What does the Bible say? It says "…For all that is in the world THE LUST OF THE FLESH [craving for sensual gratification] and THE LUST OF THE EYES [greedy longings of the mind] and THE PRIDE OF LIFE [assurance in one's own resources or in the stability of earthly things] these do not come from the Father, but are from the world [itself].

What the Bible means by the things in the world is, the lust of the flesh, the lust of the eyes, and the pride of life.

These are the core things the Bible tells us not to have, and not to desire anything that will produce the lust of the flesh, the lust of the eyes and the pride of life. It also means by implication that any desire you have on anything; whether cars, houses, clothing, school, chain watch, cap, make up and so on that will produce the lust of the flesh, or the lust of the eyes, or the pride of life in you is sin, so avoid it.

Many believers, are so tempted with these things saying, "what shall we wear?" "What shall we drive?" "What shall we eat?"There are evils in that temptation going with that season. If any man wants to be like others, if you have not purged yourself from these three basic categories of lust, you will find yourself tempted. That is why Jesus said:

 "Therefore I tell you, stop being perpetually uneasy (anxious and worried) about your life, what you shall eat or what you shall drink; or about your body, what you shall put on. Is not life greater [in quality] than food, and the body [far above and more excellent] than clothing? Matthew 6:25 (Amplified version)

Then it came to verse 32 to 34 and said:
"For the gentiles (heathen) wish for and crave and diligently seek all these things, and your heavenly Father knows well that you need them all.

But seek (aim at and strive after) first of His entire kingdom and His righteousness (His ways of doing and being right), and then all these things taken together will be given you besides. So do not worry or be anxious about tomorrow, for tomorrow will have worries and anxieties of its own. Sufficient for each day is its own trouble."

I have quoted this scripture in the Amplified version of the Bible, and it is very explanatory. Get the last phrase ". . . sufficient for each day is its own trouble". It means each day has its own trouble. NEVER lust after vanities so that the trouble of the day will not come upon you. Jesus Christ said that God knows you are in need of these things. If He knows you need them, then why worry? Just commit it to prayer and avoid lusting, then He will bring it your way. The Bible puts it this way ;"through prayer and supplication, let your request be made known to God". It is not through worry, competition and lust. Worry will bring temptation and temptation will bring death!

Aim of Temptation
The aim or target of every temptation is to bring spiritual death to you. It is to make you lose your faith, fall in to guilt and become self condemned.

*"But every person is tempted when he is drawn away, enticed and baited by his own evil desire (lust, passion).Then the evil desire, when it has conceived, gives birth to sin, and sin, when it is fully matured, brings forth death."*James 1:14-15 (Amplified version)

Whenever you are tempted by your lust, know certainly, that temptation wants to bring you to spiritual death!

Some practical steps to avoiding and overcoming temptation:

1. **Don't go nearer what tempts you.** For instance, if your friends smoke, and every time you go among them, they offer you a stick of cigarette, then avoid them and make new friends.

2. **Destroy your slippery points:** What I mean by slippery points are those materials and things that whenever you come in contact with them, you fall into sin. They are such overwhelming influence. Examples are pornographic materials, alcohols in your possession, illegal ammunition, magical books and many more things like that. If you just got saved from robbery, gangsterism or cultism - you should first of all destroy your ammunition and charms and end that chapter of temptation. If you don't deliberately and completely destroy them, those things will lead you back to the very state of a sinner again. Say God forbid!

3. **Renew your mind:** You renew your mind by your thought pattern, what dominates the mind, controls the man. I repeat it, what dominates the mind controls the man. You have to renew your mind and dominate it with good thoughts. To do this, you have to daily meditate on the word of God to have it dominate your mind. Think on holy things, thereby you will renew your mind.

Infact, the Bible is such a complete book. It even told us what to think on.

> *"Finally, brethren, whatsoever things are true, whatsoever things are honest, whatsoever things are just, whatsoever things are pure, whatsoever things are lovely, whatsoever things are of good report; if there be any virtue, and if there be any praise, think on these things".*
> Philippians 4:8 (KJV)

What do I do when I fail in temptation?

Note this that any temptation that comes to a believer is such that the believer is able to overcome. God will not allow a temptation that is bigger than you to come to you.

However, some people, because at certain points of their laxity and spiritual weakness, are not careful to apply godly principles to withstand common temptations, so they fall. God did not design us to fall in temptation, but to stand strong.

However, when you fall to one temptation does not imply the end of your Christian walk with God. It is what you do after your fall that will determine if you will continue in the life of God or not. Some people, when they fall into error, the first thing they do is to run away from their pastors or leaders. That is the wrong thing to do. It is like somebody that is injured or sick, and seeing his doctor, runs away. Are you supposed to run from your doctor when you are sick or run to him?

If you say "my sickness is an infection on my breast, I'm ashamed to show my doctor my breast for a cure" what do you think will happen to such a one? He or she may develop breast inflammation or even worst - breast cancer, and die.

So the first thing you do when you sin is to kneel immediately and confess that sin to God and receive forgiveness. There is a provision for forgiveness for us. "If we confess our sin, He is faithful and just to forgive us all our unrighteousness". This is the first and foremost thing we must do, and you must ask for forgiveness with a repentant heart.

Then, the second and very important thing you must do is that you must go to your pastor or your spiritual leader and tell him or her the truth about your temptation, and how you failed.

you must go to your pastor or your spiritual leader and tell him or her the truth about your temptation, and how you failed.

Do you know that if a man lies to his doctor, he

dies in that sickness? If a man lies to his lawyer, he loses his case, if a man lies to his pastor, he loses eternal life. Your pastor, fellowship head, spiritual leader or any matured Christian around you will be in a position to heal your spiritual backsliding, pray for you and tell you what you must do.

Summary
Remember that temptation itself is not sin, but yielding to temptation is the sin. No temptation coming upon a man is bigger than the man. Remember that you are tempted because of your own lust. Remember that you can renew your mind and overcome temptations. Remember that God does not tempt, but Satan tempts us with our lust. Remember the practical steps to avoiding temptation. And very importantly, remember to run first to your spiritual leader and tell him your weaknesses whenever you fall into temptation.

Memory Verse
You must commit this to memory and recite it closing your book: James 1:13

"Let no one say when he is tempted, "I am tempted by God"; for God cannot be tempted by evil, nor does He Himself tempt anyone.""

Exercise

1.   List the three categories of temptation Satan tempted Jesus
    With:

(i) ....

(ii)..

(iii)...

2. What are you suppose to do when you fall into   sin?...

....

....

....

3 | GROWING IN GRACE

If you happen to see a child that is three years old, and the child is not walking, what will you say? You will say "this child is not growing". It is expected that every child that is born in God's kingdom should grow spiritually, that is what it means to grow in grace.

When you grow in God's word, in prayer, in the fellowship of the saints and in evangelism, then you are growing in grace.

Do you know that for a baby to grow healthy, he/she needs a well ventilated environment full of oxygen, the breast milk, he/she also needs a very close presence of the mother, and the child on his/her own communicates through crying to remain healthy? In the same way, prayer is a spiritual atmosphere of a new believer, God's word is the breast milk of the new Christian, fellowship of the saints is the presence of the mother, and evangelism is the communicating language of the baby. Let's put it in a block

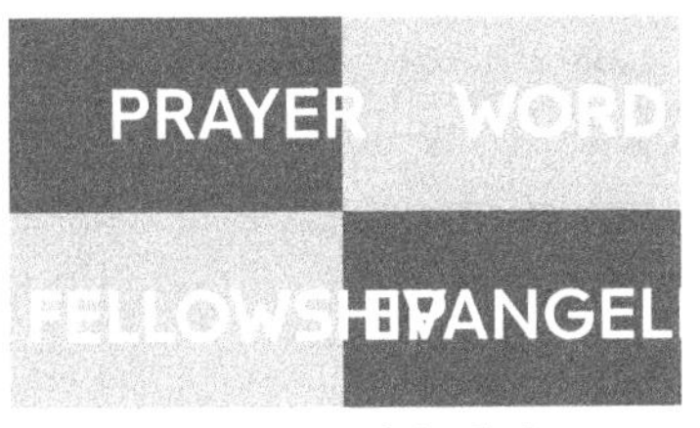

Growth block of the believer

PRAYER

Some people say prayer is talking to God but that is incomplete. Prayer means communicating with the Spirit of God. That is you talk to God, God talks back to you by His Spirit in your inner man. Prayer is the oxygen of life of every believer whether new born Christian or old. When prayer is lacking, the soul of the Christian becomes dry like a wilderness. Soon it dies for lack of spiritual oxygen. Bible says that Jesus taught them a parable that men ought always to prayer and not to faint. It means that if you are not praying, you are fainting.

How should a believer pray?

For a new believer, there is a standardized way of praying. It is called the ACTS(principle of prayer). ACTS means:

A =Adoration, C = Confession
T = Thanksgiving and   S = Supplication.

Adoration

In adoration, you should take time to worship God with songs of praise. You can lie down on the floor praying, or kneeling, or standing, raising up holy hands .You sing worship songs. From the moment you start with the worship song your prayer has stated.

Confession

Many people have misconceptions about what we confess. They say we confess our sins. That is not all about confession. It is not always that a believer confesses his sins. If you confess your sin always, then you are in a habitual state of sin that means you are a sinner. The Bible tells us again what to confess, You confess the Lordship of Jesus. You confess your faith in Him. You confess who you are in Christ Jesus. I give you an example:

"Oh! Lord, today I see Jesus Christ Lord over my soul. I declare and confess that my sins are forgiven. I am a new man. Old things are passed away. You have redeemed me by the precious blood of your sacrifice. I confess your kingship over my life. I declare that I am sitting in heavenly places with Christ Jesus. I confess I am a child of God, born of the Spirit of life".

This is the way your confession should go. However, if you have any guilt or knowledge of sin, confess it first and ask for forgiveness before you begin the confession of who you are in Christ Jesus.

Thanksgiving

When you are true with your confessions of faith, begin to thank God again for all the things He has done for you. Most especially, thank Him for saving your soul, and making you a child of God. You can sing songs here again. Some even cry out of emotions when they remember God's faithfulness. There is nothing wrong with that.

Supplication

Every child of God has a need. In Supplication, you begin to itemize your needs before God. However, I want you to see and practice supplication from a scriptural point. So many people, when they kneel to pray, all you hear is something like this:

"My Father, please give me money to purchase that cloth I told you about. Give me also money to buy that electronics. Remember to send me money for my house rent. Yes Lord, remember to grant me success in that exam I took. I also need a change of phone, please send it to me. Finally Father, give me N 750 recharge card today to call my spouse".

You see, all you see in this kind of prayer is I, me, myself and my own, so selfish a prayer. There is no place for the kingdom of God here. Jesus said:

"But seek first the kingdom of God and His righteousness, and all these things shall be added to you." Matthew 6:33

Example of good Kingdom supplication is this: "Lord, I ask of you to arise in your power and defend the missionaries in the field. Pastor P has been encountering persecutions from the heathen, please Lord give him the grace to follow. Lord, let your Spirit move in this community and save many sinners unto Christ. This is Your will. Lord, I also ask, that you will give me money to help me buy shirts so that I will not be a disgrace to your work by being un-kempt. Cause me also to pass my exams to your own glory".

You see, this second supplication has the kingdom of God in its content. That is how your prayer should be.

How often should I pray?

You pray every day. You pray very early in the morning, you pray at noon, and you pray at bedtimes. The Bible tells us about Jesus Christ, that early in the morning before the dawn, he went up the mountain to pray. You can pray also at any other time when children and activities will not distract you. Distraction is an obstacle to fervent prayer. SWITCH OFF

YOUR PHONE WHEN YOU PRAY.
"Pray without ceasing." 1Thessalonians 5:17

THE WORD:
The Bible says, "As newborn babes, desire the pure milk of the word, that you may grow thereby" 1 Peter 2: 2 .The word of God is the food of the believer, if you refuse to take it on daily basis as food, you will die of spiritual malnutrition. No new believer should be found at any place without a copy of the Bible with him or her.

As a newborn Christian, you are advice to start studying the Bible from the gospel of John. This is because the gospel of John has more of the words of Christ than any other book in the Bible. It also talks so much of the Love of Christ than any other book in the Bible. Read one chapter in the morning, one chapter in the afternoon, and one chapter at night. When you are through with the gospel of John, go to Matthew and read it through revelation in the same sequence. If you do this for six months, you will be four times a more spiritual and matured Christian than someone who did not do that. It is like a baby that is fed on powerful nutrients and another that is fed on chaff. The difference between the two babies will be obvious.

Through revelation in that sequence. If you do

this for six months, you will be a more spiritual and matured Christian than someone who did not do that. It is like a baby that is fed on powerful nutrients and another that is fed on chaff. The difference between the two babies will be obvious.

FELLOWSHIP

I want to ask you a question. If a baby is born, thereafter, the mother dies; will you take the baby that is alive and place him/her on the arms of the dead mother because she is the mother? No, you wouldn't do that, if you do that, then you are stupid. What you will do is to quickly look for another living and healthy woman who can nurse the baby.

In the same vein, if you use to have fellowship with a church that is spiritually dead, you must break that fellowship and locate a church that is spiritually vibrant for your spiritual nurturing. This is very important. Some people are afraid to change from unbiblical satanic churches. They say, "It is my parent's church". Will you allow your parent's church that is dead to frustrate your eternal destiny? Destinies are personal things. We tell people this: if your church cannot change you, change your church to a lively spiritual church that will understand the value of your soul.

How do I identify a dead church?
1. Any church that does not preach salvation from sin and does not emphasize on being born again is dead.
2. Any church that does not believe in the Holy Ghost and His gifts is dead.
3. Any church that is not forceful on evangelism is dead.

If you remain with a dead church, you will be a dead child. However, because of the great revivals that are spreading through all denominations, some so called dead churches now have Pentecostal groups for the nurture of souls. Some groups are also non denominational, and greatly doing the work in caring for new converts. I recommend such groups like Scripture Union, EFAC, NIFES, CASOR, Full Gospel Business Men Fellowship, etc. These groups have wide spread and they can help you grow.

Scripture Union, EFAC, NIFES, CASOR, Full Gospel Business Men Fellowship, etc. These groups have wide spread and they can help you grow.

The Bible says "Do not neglect the fellowship of the brethren as some people's manners are".

As a new born believer, you must disassociate from every fellowship of gangsters, beer parlours, and gossip unit. Join FULLY in the fellowship of the people of God. You must make new friends. How do you make new friends in the fellowship of God? Walk up to somebody, greet the person, introduce yourself to the person and ask for the person's name.

New fellowship sets in. Welcome to the family of God. A spiritual family, I know you will enjoy this fellowship. IT IS IMPOSSIBLE FOR YOU TO BE A BELIEVER WITHOUT THE FELLOWSHIP OF THE SAINTS. Can a branch of mango tree live on its own without the entire tree? No, it will die. You cannot be a believer without a lively church or fellowship. You will just die spiritually. If you gave your live to Christ in any of our Freedom and Healing Crusade, identify any of the churches that participated fully in the crusade, prayerfully locate one that your spirit leads you to, and be a member there. This is very important for your spiritual growth.

EVANGELISM
Evangelism means sharing the good news of Christ' power to safe someone else. The biggest testimony of Christ you can give is the testimony of how He saved you. Tell someone that you are saved and try to get the person to Christ. Jesus said that He will confess before His father anyone that confesses Him before another. Never let a day pass you by without

witnessing for Jesus Christ. Drop this book now; find someone to tell about Jesus Christ.

Do it now!

Tell someone how you got saved. Jesus is always happy with those that preach Him. Infact, the Bible says that those that convert sinners to God will shine like stars in heaven. What a glory! Become a soul winner today, convert somebody and increase your star.

glory! Become a soul winner today, convert somebody and increase your star.

Exercise:

1. Outline the four cardinal things one must do to grow in grace

....

....

....

....

....

2. Complete this statement, If you make the burden of Jesus Christ your burden, then...

3. Quote 1 Thessalonians 5;17........................

4. In the ACTS principle of prayer, "T" signifies...

5. If you want to increase your star, what do you do? ....

....

....

4 | THE HOLY SPIRIT

The most important subject in the world for a believer is the Holy Spirit. This chapter is an introduction to this most important personality on earth. The Holy Spirit is a person. He is the third person in Trinity. In the beginning of creation, when God said "Let there be light", the Holy Spirit was that Person that executed every act of creation. 7 points you should know about the Holy Spirit:

- The Holy Spirit is a person, He is a divine personality.
- The Holy Spirit Has feelings; He can bear your burdens and understands the way you feel.
- The Holy Spirit speaks. He speaks with an authoritative voice from within you; at times His voice can be so loud that you think someone physical spoke to you.
- The Holy Spirit can lead. He can direct you were to go, were not to go, what to do, what to say, etc.
- The Holy Spirit can be grieved. You can injure Him and make Him grieve. This

happens when you disobey Him or when you fall into sin.

- Without the Holy Ghost you cannot be raptured. He is the seal of our Redemption.
- The Holy Spirit is the greatest power on earth. All the power that Jesus Christ exhibited was the power of the Holy Spirit. (See Acts 10: 38), No power can operate were the Holy Spirit operates.

The subject of the Holy Spirit is so large that we cannot even exhaust its discussion in a thousand page text book. But I want you to get the elementary experience of Him for your new Christian walk.

There are two categories of things that are very important to you as a new believer. These are the fruits of the Holy Spirit and the gifts of the Holy Spirit. They are two different things. But you need them so badly like a sardine will need water. Do you know that Jesus gave us an invitation to come to the experience of the Holy Spirit? Look at how He puts it. He said:

"…If any one thirst, let him come to Me and drink. He who believes in Me, as the Scripture has said, out of his heart will flow rivers of living water." John 7:37- 38. This river of living water is the Holy Spirit and all He can give to a believer. Let's see what He can give:

THE FRUITS OF THE HOLY SPIRIT

The fruits of the Holy Spirit are the values, qualities and works which the presence of the Holy Spirit accomplishes in the life of a believer. Fruits are the most precious things in a tree or a plant. So the fruits of the Holy Spirit are the most precious value a Christian will ever have.

There are nine fruits of the Holy Spirit. You must remember the nine of them. They are: LOVE, JOY, PEACE, LONGSUFFERING, GENTLENESS, GOODNESS, FAITH, MEEKNESS and TEMPERANCE.

You know that some people club, do all sorts of sexual abominations, and call it love. That is not love, but lust. Lust makes people lost in a wild life. Love protects, is sincere, is not selfish, is not envious, and is not sinful. Love is of God, lust is of the devil. Anyone that has these fruits of the Holy Spirit in his/her life will manifest love, joy, peace, longsuffering and others.

Longsuffering means having patience. Hence forth, you must ask the Holy Spirit to give you patience as you relate to men, Goodness means you will exhibit a character of benevolence - being good to people and helping people.
It is only the Holy Ghost that can make you good to people.

Meekness is a great virtue. Meekness does not mean weakness. God is a friend to meek people? The Bible says that God resists the proud and gives grace to the humble. God gave Moses so much grace to become the greatest man in the Old Testament because he was the meekest man in his time. In heaven, humility is of a great price. Don't be proud. If pride is a family trend you have, ask God to give you a new birth and to destroy that spirit of pride.

Meekness means humility. Do you know that God is a friend to meek people? The Bible says that God resists the proud and gives grace to the humble. God gave Moses so much grace to become the greatest man in the Old Testament because he was the meekest man in his time. In heaven, humility is of a great price. Don't be proud. If pride is a family trend you have, ask God to give you a new birth and to destroy that spirit of pride.

Temperance means self control. Of course you know so many people do not have self control. They can fight and quarrel in the market place. They can be so angry, so violent, and these once behave like animals, even the way they talk. They lack temperance or self control. They can curse people as they drive. They always strive. They lack the fruits of the Spirit.

These nine fruits are very essential for everyday living as a Christian. You need these fruits to be a good matured spiritual Christian. When you come to a tree, say corn, or peer, or orange, the first thing that you admire in it is its fruits. Fruits make a tree valuable and admirable. In the same way, when we display these fruits of the Holy Spirit, we are then proper/true believers, and we are admired by men for it. The fruits of the Holy Spirit make you a True Christian.

Prayer: "Lord Jesus, put in me these sweet and wonderful fruits of the Holy Spirit".

I want you to pray this prayer for yourself for nine days.

THE GIFTS OF THE HOLY SPIRIT
Gifts of Holy Spirit are special endowments of supernatural energy given to people to do certain special works for God.

There are nine gifts of the Holy Spirit also. Do you remember that we also have nine fruits of the Holy Spirit? The fruits of the Holy Spirit make you a quality Christian, whereas the gifts of the Holy Spirit make you an effective Christian. The gifts are used for service whereas the fruits are used for personal daily living.

The gifts of the Holy Spirit are: Word of Wisdom, Word of Knowledge, Faith, Healing, Working of Miracles, Prophecy, Discerning of Spirits, Diverse kind of Tongues, and Interpretation of Tongues.

Pick up your Bible and read 1 Corinthians 12:1 - 10.

These gifts of the Spirits are divided into three bulk groups.

1) The Revelation Gifts
2) The Power Gifts
3) The Vocal Gifts

Revelation gifts give the possessor of it insight into things that are not known or discern by the human mind or senses.

Word of Wisdom: This is a divine revelation in the mind of God concerning people, places or things, always referring to the future. Have you ever being in a crusade or meeting when a preacher begins to operate in the Holy Ghost, and he or she begins to tell you or the audience what the Spirit of God says will happen to somebody? That is Word of Wisdom.

Word of Knowledge: This is also a divine revelation in the mind of God concerning people, places or things, with respect to the past or immediate presence. This gift is almost the same with the Word of Wisdom only that Word of Wisdom always talks concerning the future of people, while Word of Knowledge reveals the past or the hidden things currently happening with people. If somebody comes to a programme and suddenly begins to say something like this: "There is a woman here who has cancer of the breast, the Lord has healed you" that is Word of Knowledge.

happening with people. By word of knowledge, in a particular crusade , I said, "Someone here has an ear problem , you can't hear well with it, come out let me pray for you." Nobody responded . I got the message clearer and said, "you are a male!" Still nobody responded .More insight came to me and I said, " you have this problem in you left ear and you are 13 years old." The boy stood up and rushed to the altar holding his left ear. That is word of knowledge in operation.

In another crusade, I said by word of knowledge, "there is a lady in this meeting, you have an elder sister who is sitting right there with you. Your elder sister's name is Nkechi ; both of you have serious marital problems. Both ladies came forth, and Nkechi testified of how she had got 20 suitors, yet no one married her. That is a family curse that God Identified. Discerning of Spirit : Discerning of spirits means seeing and hearing from the Spirit realm. It is somebody hearing a voice that is not human, or seeing angels or demons, and declaring what he sees. It is a kind of spiritual vision. The Holy Ghost gives this ability to the believer if he asks for it.

These three make up the revelation gifts.

Faith: Faith is both a gift and a fruit of the Holy Spirit. The gift of faith is a supernatural knowledge and confidence in the ability of God to do a thing at that time. The operator of this gift is emboldened by a sudden consciousness that God is about to do a thing. That is the gift of faith. It works miracles.

Healing: Gifts of healing is a divine ability to cure a diseased body. Somebody who has this gift can lay hands on somebody who is sick of any kind of disease and get them healed. God can give this gift to you if you ask.

Working of Miracles: Gift of Working of Miracles is the divine ability by the Holy Spirit to recreate. The person that has this gift will not just heal disease tissues, but can recreate. Somebody that is born without eye balls can suddenly have eye balls in his eye socket by this gift. The cripple can walk by it.

These last 3 make up the power gifts. The final group of the gifts of the Holy Spirit is the vocal gifts. These gifts enable the possessor to release divine utterances. The carrier of this gift speaks mysteries, interprets mysteries, and speaks like an oracle of God. Among them are:

Diverse Tongues: This is a compulsory gift for every believer in Jesus Christ. Most times, it is the first gift a believer receives. It is called speaking in tongues. Speaking in tongues is a divine ability given to somebody to speak a language you never learnt. It could be a heavenly language or earthly language, so long as you never learnt it, but you were empowered by the Holy Spirit to speak it forth, then you are operating on a gift called diverse kind of tongues. Jesus said:
> *"And these signs will follow those who believe: In My name they will cast out demons; they will speak with new tongues."*Mark 16:17

The first gift you should seek from the Holy Spirit is to speak in tongues. Speaking in tongues is a physical evidence that you are filled with the Holy Spirit. The second most important experience you should have is the in filling with Holy Spirit evidenced by speaking in tongues.

7 things happen to you when you are filled with the Holy Spirit;
¤ You speak in tongues.
¤ You become bold.
¤ You gain more power over the devil.
¤ You pray better.
¤ You are introduced to the Spirit realm.
¤ You become a strong Christian.
¤ You carry an invisible protective flame of fire.

This invisible protective flame makes evil spirits, sorcerers, cultists, witches and wizards to quickly identify you as dangerous! Glory to God! When they go to their covens to invoke you, they are embarrassed by this protective flame that makes you untouchable.

If you are not filled with the Holy Ghost, take a fasting and praying time asking the Lord to fill you to fullness.

Interpretation of Tongues: This is a divine ability to have understanding of the meaning of a language being spoken in tongues. Many people speak in tongues, but just a few interpret. If you ask for it, Jesus can give it to you.

Prophecy: Prophecy is inspired utterance that brings correction, exhortation or rebuke to the people of God. Everybody that God gives the Spirit of prophecy uses that same gift to serve the body of Christ. Look at how the gift of prophecy operates: you may be in a fellowship or a church service, prayer begins to go up, high and high. You suddenly see somebody beginning to speak out loud to everybody, as though the Spirit has just given a message for everybody. He begins to speak out this message under divine unction. This is prophecy, the simple gift of prophecy. When somebody prophesies it does not automatically mean the person is a prophet. Not at all. There are many more things it takes for a person to be a prophet. A prophet will definitely prophesy, but he must of necessity have two or three of the revelation gifts coupled with prophecy for him to be a prophet. Don't be discouraged when you see yourself only prophesying, God can equally give you the other gifts and make you a prophet.

Little Exercise
Take a pen and mark the 3 most essential gifts of the Holy Spirit you desire to have within 6 months.
Word of wisdom☐ Faith ☐ Diverse Tongues ☐

Word of knowledge ☐ Healing ☐ interpretation of tongues ☐

Discerning of spirits ☐   Miracles ☐ Prophecy ☐

Having marked them, pray every day of your life for them: Jesus is willing to give you even all of them. Look at what He said:
"If you then been evil know how to give good gifts to your children, how much more will your heavenly Father give the Holy Spirit to those who ask Him" Luke 11;13

The Leading of the Holy Spirit:

When Jesus was going out of the earth, He said He will send us another comforter who will be with us FOREVER. Immediately Christ left, He sent the Holy Spirit who came on the day of Pentecost and dwelled with the early disciples. Since then, He has never left the earth. That is the good news. That same Holy Ghost has been directing and leading the people of God. When you are lead by the Holy Spirit you have peace in that matter, when he is not leading you, you are in strong doubt and worry.

Where does the Holy Ghost live?

The Holy Spirit does not live on trees or in houses, He lives in men. That is why the Bible says "your body is the temple of the Holy Spirit." When you live in sin, you drive out the Holy Spirit who lives in you; you destroy His temple which is your body. Sin destroys the body where the Holy Ghost lives.

Jesus knew we will not be able to face Satan when He(Jesus) leaves, so He promised to send to us someone who is so powerful that when He lives in you , Satan will tremble and fear. The Holy Ghost is divine and powerful.

When you receive the Holy Ghost in filling, then you become a conquering Christian immediately.

When you become born again and you are filled with the Holy Spirit, the Holy Spirit immediately begins to guide and lead you. He begins to instruct you, and restrain you from doing certain things. He begins to wake you up to pray. He begins to direct you where you should go and find good believers. This work of the Holy Spirit is what we call being lead by the Spirit.

Practical Guides to Know How He leads:
1. When He leads, you have peace on that way in your inner man.
2. When you experience worry and anxiety within you, the Holy Spirit is not leading you to that direction.
3. When He leads, you have no fear.
4. When He leads, what He tells you to do is always in line with the bible.
5. He can lead you by giving you an instruction from the bible.
6. He can lead you by making you hear a song

that will inspire you to a spiritual action.
7.   When He leads you, you understand the ways of God.
8.   He does not lead you into temptation.

From today, desire that the Holy Spirit should lead you. Pray for that every day. For as many as are lead by the spirit are the sons of God.

Exercise:

1. The Holy Spirit is a person. True   False

2. The Holy Spirit can be grieved True False

3. Without the Holy Spirit you can't be raptured. True   False

4. List the nine (9) fruits of the Holy Spirit:
i.   ....
ii.   ....
iii.   ....

iv.   ....
v.   ....
vi.   ....
vii.   ....
Viii ....
Ix   ....

6. What is temperance?
....
....

7. Divine ability in the mind of God concerning

people, places

7. Divine ability in the mind of God concerning people, places and things with respect to the past or presence is called..............................

8. Inspired utterance that brings correction, exhortation, or rebuke is call............................

9. List three practical guides to know when the Holy Ghost
    leads
I)...
ii)...
iiii)...

10. The first physical evidence that you have been filled with Holy Spirit is
....

5. List the nine (9) gifts of the Holy Spirit:
I..
ii...
iii..
iv...
v..
vi...
vii..
viii...
ix...

5 CHALLENGE OF CHRISTIAN LIFE

The life of a Christian is like the life of a soldier. Every soldier has hurdles, challenges, and obstacles to conquer in every field of battle. Without challenges, the soldier is just a civilian. Challenges toughen a soldier, brighten his visions and make him more determinant and strong. We are soldiers of Christ with trials and challenges on our way as we fulfill the call of Christ. But the Bible has already told us not to be discouraged when we see challenges. The Bible commands us in James 1:23 to count persecution as a thing of joy saying.

> *"My brethren, count it all joy when you fall into various trials, knowing that the testing of your faith produces patience."*

You cannot be a strong Christian if you have not gone through one form or another form of trial. Most times, believers' trials come in the form of persecution.

What is persecution?

 Persecution is when a believer is denied his fundamental right because of his faith. It could be right to freedom of access, or speech or shelter or money even life.

When Apostle Paul was persecuted, he was beaten thoroughly, yet he was not discouraged, infact he glorified in it. He listed his persecution as his badge of honor. He said:

> *"From the Jews five times I received forty stripes minus one. Three times I was*
>
> *beaten with rods; once I was stoned; three times I was shipwrecked; a night and a day I have been in the deep; in journeys often, in perils of waters, in perils of robbers, in perils of my own countrymen, in peril of the Gentiles, in peril in the city, in perils in the wilderness, in perils in the sea, in perils among false brethren; in weariness and toil, in sleeplessness often, in hunger and thirst, in fasting often, in cold and nakedness."*
>
> 2 Corinthians 11:24 27

You see, trials and persecutions can come to see how firm you are as a Christian. Your persecution can come from: Your parents or guidance, your spouse, your employer or boss, your family, your neighbor, your peers, your leaders.

The Bible says that those who want to live godliness in Christ Jesus must suffer persecution. (See 2 Timothy 3: 12). You see, persecution that comes to you because of your godliness is an honour; but when you are persecuted because you are ungodly, that is a great fall. God does not reward such persecutions. Infact, that kind is not persecution, but judgment.

You are persecuted because they are offended that you are now practicing a deeper faith in Jesus Christ. They want you to deny Christ and your new faith. But if you resist them and joyfully go through your denials, Christ will honour you. Jesus has already said, *"Blessed are you when they revile and persecute you, and say all kinds of evil against you falsely for My sake. Rejoice and be exceedingly glad, for great is your reward in heaven, for so they persecuted the prophets who were before you."* Matthew 5:11-12.

Do you know that some Christians after the times of the Apostles were thrown to lions? Lions ate them, and the heathen were entertained with that scene. Some had their bodies poured over with tar and fire kindled on them. They burned like torches all through the nights, becoming human burn-fires to entertain the heathens. Some were shot dead. Some were killed with the sword. Do you know what? None of them ever murmured going through their persecutions. When they were killed, they were smiling. So many of them were singing as they went through their death! Are you ready to die for Jesus Christ if need be? heathen were entertained with that scene. Some had their bodies poured over with tar and fire kindled on them. They burned like torches all through the nights, becoming human burn-fires to entertain the heathens. Some were shot dead. Some were killed with the sword. Do you know what? None of them ever murmured going through their persecutions. When they were killed, they were smiling. So many of them were singing as they went through their death! Are you ready to die for Jesus Christ if need be?

Paul told Timothy his spiritual son to endure hardship as a true soldier of Christ. That means hard time can come to a Christian.

Persecutions can rise from these areas:
  When they expect you to contribute to exam malpractice   and you refuse.
  When they expect you to get involve with them in rituals   and evil customs and you refuse.

When your boss demands for sex from you and you refuse.
When they expects you to bribe your way through and you refuse.
When they expects you to fornicate or commit adultery and   you refuse.

Any of these things can stir up hatred against you because of your faith. But the Bible has told us that he that endures unto the end shall be saved.

What Do I do When I'm Persecuted?
Never be angry with the persecutor, rather pray for him or her (open your Bible to Matthew 5:44, read it now!)

Rejoice and be thankful to God that you are persecuted. Be fervent in prayer. You will win. Let the brethren know what you are passing through.

Never compromise your faith!
What is the Reward of Enduring Persecution?

A great eternal reward in heaven.
You will become a stronger Christian. You will enjoy a closer fellowship with God.
With these lessons, you now understand that persecutions are not evil, but necessary to make the Christian soldier strong. If you meet it, embrace it, and keep on.
Memory verse - 1 Peter 4:16

"Yet if any man suffer as a Christian, let him not be ashamed, but let him glorify God in this matter."

EXERCISE

1) From the Bible, list four persons you know were persecuted in the New Testament:
    i..
    ii...
    iii..
    iv...

2) Persecution makes us to be a weak Christian.
    True   False

3) Can hard times come to a Christian?
    ....

4) Quote James 1:2&3

5) List five things you must do when passing through persecution:
    I. ....
    ii...
    iii..
    iv...
    v..

6) Is persecution part of the Christian package? (See 2 Timothy 3:11, Mark 10:30)...................................

6 | SPIRITUAL WARFARE

One of the greatest generals of God in history is Apostle Paul. Apostle Paul fought many spiritual battles for Christ that he even said that he fought with beasts at Ephesus. He overcame in spiritual warfare because he knew the tactics to overcome Satan. One of his greatest statements concerning spiritual warfare is this; I quote:

"For we wrestle not against flesh and blood, but against principalities, against powers, against the rulers of the darkness of this world, against spiritual wickedness in high places". Whaoh!

That means we are wrestling, we are fighting, we are in a battle. The day we were born again, we were born into a spiritual warfare. Our enemies are principalities, powers of darkness, evil spiritual rulers, and satanic wickedness in high places. These are all agents of Satan. They are our enemies, and we are their enemies. If they see a way to kill us, they will kill us. But if we remain in Christ, the wicked one cannot touch us, because it is written *"you are of God, little children, and have overcome them, because, He who is in you is GREATER than he who is in the world."*1 John 4;4. Who is he that is in the world? It is Satan, principalities, demons, witches, rulers of darkness. Who is He that is in us? Can you guess who? It is Christ Jesus of course! The Bible puts it like this:*"CHRIST IN YOU, THE HOPE OF GLORY"Now say it loud and clear! "Christ in me, the hope of glory"*

This will make you not to be afraid of spiritual warfare because greater is He that is in you, than he that is in the world.

I will tell you a story about Elisha.

Elisha was a mighty prophet in the Bible. He is one of the mightiest prophets. One day, a king came to fight against the King of Israel. Elisha by revelation (you remember what we taught about the revelation gifts?), Elisha used that to know where this enemy king was and knew how to defeat him. So Elisha told the king of Israel where the enemy king was and how to defeat him. The enemy was surprised at how the king of Israel knew this. The enemy changed location, and Elisha still knew and told the king of Israel. Again, the enemy was defeated, and it repeated the third time. The enemy became so discouraged that he asked his men "who is betraying us and telling the king of Israel our secrets?". One of his elite soldier and counselor told him, that it is nobody, but Elisha the prophet of Israel; that this Elisha tells the king of Israel everything about him, even the things he does in his private rooms.

So the enemy king decided to arrest Elisha. He took with him a great army of horses and chariots to Elisha's house at night.

Gahazi, the servant of Elisha came out in the night to ease himself, lo and behold; he saw the entire surroundings occupied with enemy forces. He ran in and told Elisha who alone was in the room that they were finished. However, Elisha told him not to be afraid of this great enemy army because they have more forces with them than that which is with the enemy. Elisha then prayed and asked God to open his servant's eyes so that he will see the armies of God that are with them.

Suddenly, Gehazi's eyes open, and he saw very great army, greater than the enemy's forces that are with them. This army he saw had horses and chariots, the enemy forces is not a match to this army. Do you know what? Elisha and his servant Gehazi arrested that entire enemy multitude! Interesting!! Isn't it?

This is because God was with them. In spiritual warfare, you don't normally see the angels with you, but they are always there to protect you from harm.

Who do we fight?

We fight forces of darkness that make men to refuse the gospel of Jesus Christ. We fight occult powers that enslave destinies of men. We fight demons of hell that afflict people with diseases. We fight against the powers that spread sin.

The Weapon of Our Warfare

World armies use machine guns, AK 47, rocket launchers, grenades and armoured tanks in every conventional warfare. These are their weapons. In spiritual warfare, we also have weapons, very powerful weapons. These weapons are spiritually designed to incapacitate demons. The Bible says: "For the weapons of our warfare are not carnal but mighty in God for pulling down strongholds, casting down arguments and every high thing that exalts itself against the knowledge of God, bringing every thought into captivity to the obedience of Christ."2 Corinthians 10:4-5.

Devils dwell in colonies and in kingdoms. Some dwell in the astral world, some in water world, and some in the air. But do you know what? Our weapons of warfare can

destroy an entire satanic colony in a region. A warring Christian is very, very dangerous to Satan. Some of the most deadly weapons of our warfare are:
•   The Blood of Jesus
•   The Word of God
•   The Weapon of Praise
•   Holy Ghost Fire
•   Speaking in Tongues

When you are in emergency, and you scream, THE BLOOD OF JESUS, Something happens. Something mighty happens. The blood of Jesus will be released in the Spirit realm to shield you from danger, and that same blood is highly corrosive to the enemy. That blood that shields you is corrosive, like acid, to powers of darkness. For instance, we know that salt is an essential mineral for our bodies;

Isn't it? We leak it with our soft tongue, and feel alright, but that same salt touching the body of an earth worm kills it immediately. It corrodes the body of the earth worm, no matter how big the earth warm is, salt kills it. Such is the blood of Jesus to demons. The same blood we take as communion corrodes the bodies of demons. No matter how big the demon looks.

Even angel Michael used the blood of Jesus to defeat Satan. The Bible made us to know that when Michael the arch angel fought Satan, Michael found it very difficult to prevail.

Suddenly, he remembered the blood of Jesus, and used it against Satan. The Bible said concerning that war: "And they (Michael and the angels) overcame him (Satan) by the blood of the Lamb and by the word of their testimony".

The Word of God
The Bible says Michael overcame Satan by the blood of the Lamb, and the word of their testimony. The word of their testimony is the Word of God. You remember that when Satan tempted Jesus in the wilderness, Jesus was always saying "It is written." Satan knows that what is written is a law. When you quote the Word of God to Satan, he trembles, because the Word of God is God himself. Let me give you example of how to use the Word of God to defeat Satan:
"Satan in the name of Jesus, I exercise the authority that is vested on the Word of God. It is written; whatsoever you shall bind on earth shall be bound in heaven. Therefore, you evil powers troubling this place, I bind you, and dethrone you in Jesus name".

Devil at that time recognizes that what you are quoting is real, and he flees from you.

The Weapon of Praise.
Praise is a mighty instrument of battle. You bring God into the battle when you praise.

If you wake up in the middle of the night and begin to praise intensely, then you are very dangerous to Satan and his cohorts. There was this king in the Bible, his name is Jehoshaphat. He was a king of Judah. Some armies came up to war against him, the armies of the Moabites, the Ammonites and others. These armies were so great that Jehoshaphat was afraid, and prayed with all Israel. On the day of the battle, Jehoshaphat took singers, people that can praise the Lord, set them before his army. As these singers began to praise the Lord and say "praise the Lord, for His mercy endures forever." God rose and fought Jehoshaphat's battles for him. God caused those enemy kings, the three of their armies to slaughter each other. That was victory, Jehoshaphat only sang praises and God did the wars! See it in 2 Chronicles 20:1 25.

dangerous to Satan and his cohorts. There was this king in the Bible, his name is Jehoshaphat. He was a king of Judah. Some armies came up to war against him, the armies of the Moabites, the Ammonites and others. These armies were so great that Jehoshaphat was afraid, and prayed with all Israel. On the day of the battle, Jehoshaphat took singers, people that can praise the Lord, set them before his army. As these singers began to praise the Lord and say "praise the Lord, for His mercy endures forever." God rose and fought Jehoshaphat's battles for him. God caused those enemy kings, the three of their armies to slaughter each other. That was victory, Jehoshaphat only sang praises and God did the wars! See it in 2 Chronicles 20:1 - 25.

When you sing praises, you introduce God to the war!
Nugget to Praise War:
- Sing songs that are spiritual.
- Sing songs that move your spirit.
- Sing it until it makes meaning to you.
- Make the song your prayer.
- Sing it out loud.

Holy Ghost Fire:
Have you heard people pray before and shout "Holy Ghost fire!" do you know what they are doing by that? They are invoking the most devastating supernatural fire. Holy Ghost fire burns more that a hydrogen bomb! Look at how you pray with Holy Ghost fire.
"All you power of darkness infiltrating this region with darkness, I release HOLY GHOST FIRE against you! To destroy your network, and cease your activity".
Holy Ghost fire is a weapon!

SPEAKING IN TONGUES:
Have you heard this song before?
Amen, amen we bind the devil
In Jesus power, in this place

We speak in tongues, devil is
  confused
Forever and ever! Amen!

When you speak in tongues, Satan's intellectual system reads "error". Do you know why? Because devils don't understand tongues, therefore, they can't interpret what you say. When you speak in tongues, Satan can't understand, he feels threatened, he runs. The Spirit of God understands tongues; He interprets it and applies what you just commanded against Satan. The Bible says that he that speaks in tongues speaks MYSTERIES unto God (Read 1 Corinthians 14: 2) Satan does not understand that mystery. You know that communication is a powerful tool in warfare. If your enemy understands what you are saying, they sabotage it. Brother Paul knew the secrets and power of tongues. So he wrote and said "I speak in tongues more than you all".

Speak in tongues. Blast it loud and clear! Speak that heavenly language. I can speak in tongues for hours none stop. Tongue speaking is one great secret of my ministry. Begin it from today. Will you?

The Name of Jesus
You know what God said about the name of Jesus. The Bible said that God has highly exalted his name above every other

name, that at the name Jesus, every knee must bow and every tongue must confess that Jesus Christ is Lord.(see Philippians 2;9-10)

Do you know that in Satan's kingdom they don't call that name JESUS! Any one of Satan's agents that make the mistake of calling it is punished severely. Why don't they call the name? Whenever anyone calls that name, it shakes their kingdom like bomb blast! How powerful that name is! What they call Jesus in the kingdom of darkness is "The Righteous One!" They are afraid to call the name. The Bible says God has given us right of use of His name. You can call that name. Whenever you feel satanic attack, shout "JESUS". By that, you are invoking the Spirit of our mystery Jesus. Jesus is the mystery. The Name of the Lord is a strong tower.
These weapons are the very essential weapons you will use to tackle Satan and win him.

HOW DO I ENGAGE IN SPIRITUAL WARFARE?

1. Praying and Fasting:
whenever you fast, your spiritual power increases tremendously. If you study   God's word and fast, then it increases much more.

2. Mid-night Prayers:
Witches and wizards operate at night. Occult powers gather at night. When men

sleep, demons are much more awake. Any Christian that prays between 12midnight to 3am is very dangerous to Satan. Paul and Silas prayed "At midnight" and the prison doors opened. They waited till midnight for them to address those powers of darkness that kept them on chains. Utilize these weapons and pray for the deliverance of someone you know devil has kept under chain. The chain will be broken. It may be chains of sin, or affliction or unbelief!

3. Group Prayer:

When you pray together with a believer you produce more power. Jesus said, *"Again I say to you that if two of you agree on earth concerning anything that they ask , it will be done for them by My Father in heaven."* (Matthew 18:19)

When you agree with somebody to pray for an issue, addressing the enemy forces, you make tremendous impart.

Do you have a prayer partner? You need one! It is very compulsory.

Memory verse Ephesians 6:12
"For we do not wrestle against flesh and blood, but against principalities, against powers, against the rulers of the darkness of this age, against spiritual host of

Exercise:

Complete these sentences:

1. (a) The Bible says that he that speaks in tongues speaks __________ unto God.

   (b) What they call Jesus in the kingdom of darkness is __________________

   (c) The name of the Lord is a ___________, the righteous run into it, and they ________

2. What is the name of the King of Judah that won a war by the power of praise?

   ____

3. Quote 2Chronicles 20:22

   ....

   ....

   ....

   ....

4. List the six most powerful weapon of our warfare:

   (i)__________________(ii)__________________

   (iii)________________________________

   (iv)________________(v)______________

   (vi)__________________

5. One of these is <u>not</u> a vital way to engage in spiritual warfare (Tick one that is not a vital way only)

   Praying and Fasting Church Picnic

   Midnight Prayers   Group Prayer

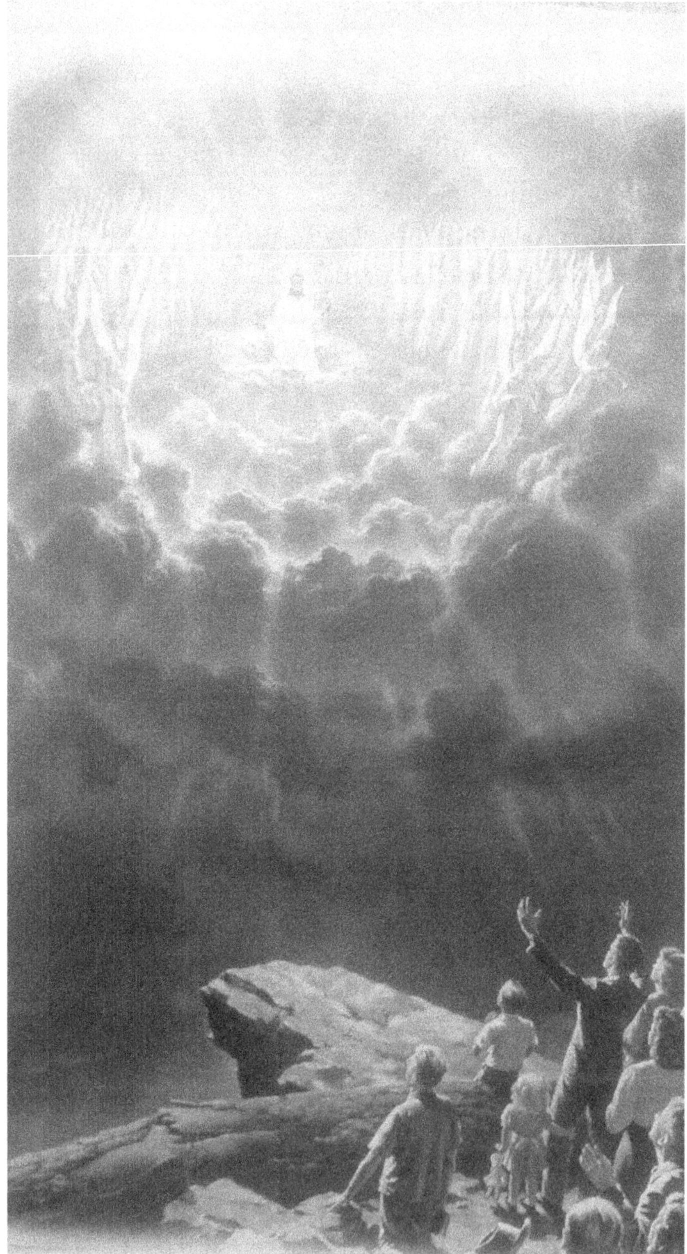

7 THE HOPE OF THE SAINTS

This chapter deals with the highest of the Christian hope, the summit of our faith that is the coming of Jesus Christ. Jesus Christ went to be with God the Father in heaven and promised every believer that He will come back to earth to take the true believers, the saints, the sanctified ones with Him to heaven. It's been about 2,000 years ago He gave that promise, and He gave us signs that will take place, that will make us know His second coming is at hand. His first coming was when He came at birth; second coming will be when He will come in the clouds with mighty angels. There are many sure, reliable and authentic words of Jesus Christ in the Holy Bible that assures us that the Messiah, Jesus Christ will come again. Among them is this one that He told His disciples saying in John 14:1-3:

> *"Let not your heart be troubled; you believe in God, believe also in Me. In My Father's house are many mansions; if it were not so, I would*

He said He will come back and that not only that He will come back, but that He will take us along side to heaven. This is a true promise, and a true statement of Christ.

Do you know that Jesus Christ went up to heaven from mount olives, in Israel? He did not disappear spontaneously. He was talking with the chosen disciples and suddenly He was been lifted from the ground, easily and gradually He was ascending, floating into air, and still preaching. Gradually, gradually ,he went and they could not see Him again. As they were still gazing to see if they could still catch a glimpse of Him, suddenly, two angels appeared to them on that very spot and this is what the angels said:

"...Men of Galilee, why do you stand gazing up into heaven? This same Jesus, who was taken up from you into heaven, will so come in like manner as you saw Him go into heaven."
Acts 1:11

This statement of the angels also matches with the statement of the prophet Enoch, which he saw many hundred years before Christ's coming. Enoch was the seventh generation from Adam, in that ancient time, he saw the Lord's coming and cried out saying:

". . . Behold, the Lord comes with ten thousands of His saints, to execute judgment on all, to convict all who are ungodly among them of all their ungodly deeds which they have ungodly committed in an ungodly way, and of all the harsh things which ungodly sinners have spoken against Him." Jude Vs 14 , 15

The Great Futuristic Experience

The greatest expectation of every believer is the taking away of the saints or the true believers from the tribulations of the earth into heaven. That taking away experience is called THE RAPTURE! Some call it, "Rapture of the saints." It's the same thing.

The Bible says that Jesus Christ will come from heaven into the cloud, and with a multitude, (what Enoch called Myriads) of His holy angels. It is a day that nobody knows. Even the greatest prophet that lives now does not know the day. It could be this night, or tomorrow morning. It can be next five years, or next seven years. Nobody knows the very time or date.

When Jesus Christ comes in the earth's cloud, the mighty Arch Angel (chief angel) will blow the great trumpet. This trumpet has supernatural energy. Every dead believer wherever they are will hear it in the land of the dead. Jesus said "the time will come when the dead will hear the voice of the son of man, and those that hear shall live."This trumpet blast will wake the dead that are long-dead in the bottom of the oceans, in many burial grounds. In battle fields, Christians that were killed by bullets and fire will suddenly rise again; from all over the world. The blacks in Africa, the red Indians, the white Europeans, everybody that is a born again Christian will wake and rise from their resting places.

Paul saw it and puts it this way in 1 Thessalonians 4:16- 17

> *"For the Lord Himself will descend from heaven with a shout, with the voice of an archangel and with the trumpet of God. And the dead in Christ will rise first. Then we who are alive and remain shall be caught up together with them in the clouds to meet the Lord in the air. And thus we shall always be with the Lord."*

If your father died a Christian, he will

wake .If any of your friends died as Christians, they will wake. This is a time of great joy to the redeemed of God. You know you are redeemed immediately you made the sinners prayer, you are redeemed. When we wake from the dead, we shall then die no more! Alleluia!

Who will be raptured?

The Bible says the dead in Christ shall rise first! That is every believer that is dead will rise. The believers that are not yet dead, you and me, will suddenly change and be raptured.

God cannot rapture this flesh. Do you know why? It is because flesh and blood cannot inherit the Kingdom of God. But suddenly, our bodies will become immortal by the Spirit of God and we will be raptured. This whole rapture will take place in less than a second! Before you blink your eyes it has happened! Paul saw it and revealed how it will happen. He said in 1Corinthians 15:50-52

> *"Now this I say, brethren, that flesh and blood cannot inherit the Kingdom of God; nor does corruption inherit incorruption. Behold, I tell you a mystery: We shall not all sleep (die), but we shall all be changed. In a moment, in the twinkling of an eye, at the last trumpet. For the trumpet will*

sound, and the dead will be raised incorruptible, and we shall be changed."

There is another resurrection that everyone will be resurrected and judged. But that is not the rapture. That one will come about a thousand years after rapture. The rapture is for the saints only. We shall put on a new body. It is the believer in Jesus Christ that will be raptured. We shall be changed! This is a remarkable experience every true believer will have.

With which Body shall we be Raptured?

The answer is there in the Bible: it says: but some man will say, How are the dead raised up? And with what body do they come? "Then the same book answered it and said:

"So also, is the resurrection of the dead. It is sown in corruption, it is raised in incorruption. It is sown in dishonor, it is raised in glory: it is sown in weakness; it is raised in power. It is sown a natural body; it is raised a spiritual body. There is a natural body and there is a spiritual body." 1 Corinthians 15:42-44 (King James Version)
natural body and there is a spiritual body." 1 Corinthians 15:42-44 (King James Version)

The answer is that we will be raptured with a spiritual body. When Jesus woke from the dead, you remembered He died with a natural body; He raised that same body from the grave, that same body was now made spiritual by the power of the Holy Ghost. There was no longer blood in that same body, because He shed all the blood on Calvary. That body was changed, or transformed to be like the body of angels, a true spiritual body, and was taken up to heaven.

You remember flesh and blood shall not inherit the Kingdom of God.

Open your arms, look at your body and arms and say it loud and clear: "YOU NATURAL BODY, YOU SHALL BE CHANGED TO A SPIRITUAL BODY TO MEET THE LORD IN THE AIR" say it again.

In the epistle, the Bible calls it quickening of our mortal bodies. It says "if the Spirit of Him that raised Jesus from the dead dwells in you, He that raised Christ from the dead shall quicken your mortal bodies, by His Spirit that dwells in you." Romans 8;11

This is the greatest transformation our bodies will experience.

Have you seen where they plant a bean

seed or even a corn? The corn becomes dead, you will even see the dead seed of the corn; and then you see another plant of corn growing out of the corn or bean seed. It is the same seed of corn or bean that is coming out as a plant! Isn't it? But it has taken a new body.

We shall be changed. You will not see your old body dropping down, but you shall be changed. When you pass an electric current through a filament of a bulb, what happens? The dull dead- looking filament suddenly grows with brilliant light in a micro-second! What a mystery! The current changed the nickel filament and made that dull thing that appears dead to give out luminous light. That is how rapture is give out luminous light. That is how rapture is.

The Holy Ghost is that current that changes our body configuration and make us light and rapturable!

THE CHANGE FACTOR

The Holy Spirit is the change factor! Without the Holy Ghost dwelling inside of you, you cannot be raptured! The Holy Spirit is so important to the believer that at the end of the age, people that do not have Him will never be raptured. The Holy Spirit quickens and transforms our mortal bodies. He is the one that makes your body a spiritual body. See another scripture: Here the Bible warned us not to make the Holy Spirit angry, because He is the seal for our redemption. If you make the Holy Ghost angry by sin, rebellion or unbelief and He leaves, then you cannot be raptured. See how the Bible says it:

> *"And do not grieve the Holy Spirit of God, by whom you were sealed for the day of redemption."*
> Ephesians 4:30

The day of redemption is the rapture day.
You know that paper cannot be magnetized by a magnet. But if you put an iron inside the paper, a magnet in the attempt to pull the iron will pull the paper. Your body is like the paper, the Holy Spirit in you is like the iron. The magnet is like the trumpet blast, that trumpet blast can attract the Holy Spirit and whatsoever the Spirit is inside of. If you put a wood inside of a paper, a magnet cannot attract that.

Now, if you are not at peace with the Holy Spirit, make peace with Him and be rapture ready. Remember, some will be left behind!

Is Rapture for 144 Thousand People Only?
 Not at all. Some ignorant people think the rapture is for 144 thousand people only. In revelation chapter 7 after John was shown 144

thousand people before the throne of God, he was also shown innumerable multitude from every tribe and country redeemed from the earth standing before that same throne of God. These are the saints that have been raptured from every country. The first 144 thousand people are the raptured elects from the nation of Isreal , the other multitude is every other believer. You are in that multitude.

How can I be ready for Rapture?
The answer is very simple, keep yourself from sin. Become the spotless bride of Christ, and always pray in the Holy Ghost. Forgive anybody that sin against you, because people that bear grudge will never be raptured. Be ready and watchful, being in harmony with God until the day of His appearance.

Dearly Beloved,

I am very happy that I have given you this truth. I'm sure that if you keep to this message, we will one day meet in the City of Christ. You have done a noble course for yourself by reading through this pages. Now do the final examination. When you are through with the final examination, tear it out and post it to the mail box below; addressing it this way;

Evangelist Ernest Uzoho
Mission Rescue Evangelistic Network
P . O . Box 448, Port Harcourt

Make sure you put your correct return address at the back of your envelop. Or email it to us at info@missionrescue.org

If you are successful in the exam, you will receive from us, a BASIC CHRISTIAN CERTIFICATE mailed to your box. I admonish you finally to be strong in the Lord and in the power of His might.

Exercise
1. What is the greatest expectation of the Christian believer?......................................
2. Will sinners partake in the rapture? ....
3. In the rapture, who will rise up first?...........
4. Something remarkable will happen to a believer's mortal body during rapture. What is that remarkable thing?............................
5. Outline three things you must do to be ready for rapture...................................
....
....
....

FINAL EXAMINATION

1. The transformative Spiritual experience a person experiences at the moment he/she gives his or her life to Christ is called________________________

2. Lists three assurances of your salvation ____________________________,________________________________

    ____

3. In two sentences, differentiate between trial and temptation.

    ____

    ____

4. The aim or objective of every temptation is to bring ____________________

5. List the four cardinal blocks that a believers must build on to grow in grace

    ________________________, ________________________, ________________and ________________

6. The biggest testimony of Christ you can give is ____________________________

7. List the nine fruits of the Holy Spirit____________________________,____________________,

    ____________________,____________________,____________________,____________________,

    ____________________,____________________,________________________________

8. Differentiate between the fruits of the Holy Spirit and the gifts of the Holy Spirit

    ____

    ____

9. Where does the Holy Spirit live? ____

10. Is persecution part of the Christian package?   Yes [ ]   No [ ]

11. In this booklet, what is the name of the King of Judah that won a war by praise

    ____

12. What is that remarkable thing that will happen to a believer mortal body during rapture?

    ____

www.ingramcontent.com/pod-product-compliance
Lightning Source LLC
Chambersburg PA
CBHW061247140726
47998CB00006B/2137